For Nate and Sophie, my most precious cargo.

~ *Tim McCanna*

Gigantic, humongous, tremendous love and thanks to Michelle,
Genevieve, Rachel and Kaelin. Without you, life would be so teeny tiny!

~ *Keith Frawley*

Little Bahalia Publishing
207 E. Buffalo Street, Suite 600
Milwaukee, Wisconsin 53202

Designed by Stacey Williams-Ng

First paperback edition, 2013

Printed in Malaysia

Library of Congress Cataloguing data on file.

ISBN 13: 978-0-9896688-1-1
ISBN 10: 0-9896688-1-9

Visit www.littlebahalia.com

Teeny tiny trucks.
Smaller than a dime.
So much to deliver, in very little time.

Revving up the engines. Ready for the day.
A teeny tiny convoy, heading far away.

"Breaker breaker, Buddy!"
"What's your twenty, Friend?"
"Pedal to the metal, and I'm coming 'round the bend!"

Teeny tiny tires. With teeny tiny treads.
Leaving teeny tiny trails between the flower beds.

Underneath the ivy. Beetles run amok!
A garden is a jungle to a teeny tiny truck.

Driving over bridges. Down a rocky pass. Deep into a valley of green and dewy grass.

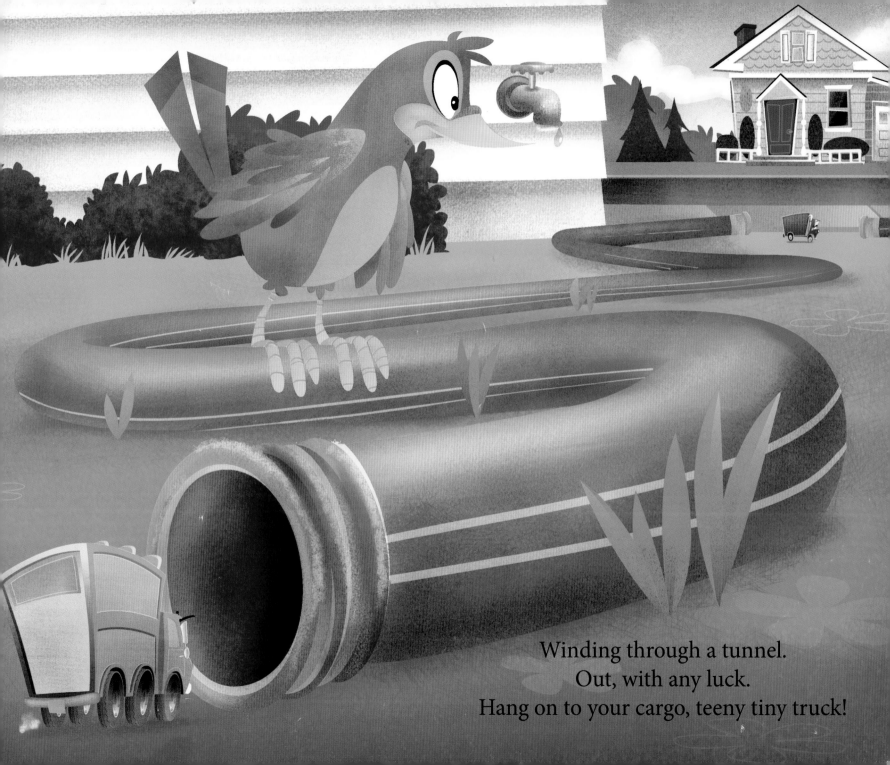

Winding through a tunnel.
Out, with any luck.
Hang on to your cargo, teeny tiny truck!

Stopping at the station.
Gotta check your weight.
Tractor-trailer hauling
twenty milligrams of freight.

Rolling on the sidewalk. Bumping over cracks.
Turn the teeny tiny wheel to navigate the jacks.

"Buddy, got your ears on?"
"Hear what Smokey said?"
"That's a big 10-4. Fender bender up ahead."

Creeping with the traffic. Running way behind!
Better take a shortcut, if there's one to find...

Parking on a lily pad. Drifting with the ducks.
A fitting way to ferry lots of teeny tiny trucks!

Reaching destinations.
Even as it rains.
Dropping little boxes
onto teeny tiny — trains!

Now the work is over. Need another load. Start again tomorrow, down another road.

Pull into a truck stop.
What a pretty sight!
Teeny tiny trucks, time to say—
"Honk Hooonk!"— Good night.

The End

Trucker Talk

Fender Bender

CARGO
Goods transported in the trailer of a truck

BREAKER-BREAKER
How truckers say, "Hey, listen up everybody!"

Breaker breaker!

FENDER BENDER
A traffic accident

PEDAL TO THE METAL
To drive very fast

SMOKEY
Policeman or sheriff in a patrol car

OVER
How truckers say, "I'm done talking. Your turn."

OVER AND OUT
Means "Good-bye, I'm hanging up now."

GOT YOUR EARS ON?
How truckers ask, "Are you listening?"

CONVOY
A group of trucks moving together on a highway.

WHAT'S YOUR 20?
How truckers ask "Where are you?"

Over and out!

That's a big 10-4!

THAT'S A BIG 10-4
How truckers say "Yes" or "Okay" or "I agree!"

TEENY TINY TRUCKS

read & play ▶

singalong ▶

LITTLE
BAHALIA
PUBLISHING

"Teeny Tiny Trucks" is also an interactive storybook app for iPad and iPhone! Enjoy playing and singing with your favorite trucks.

Available on the
App Store